"This charming book tells the story of one young woman's experience going through a Christian nursing program at the beginning of the turbulent 1960s. What she experienced often challenged her beliefs, which at their foundation was sufficient to carry her through and grow in her faith. A literary treasure!"
Virginia Kruse

"Ruth captures the challenges, stresses and joys of becoming a nurse. Most of us went to nursing school not really understanding what that meant. When we graduated, we were wiser about life than when we started."
Trish Nienow

"I graduated from nursing school in 1960 and had many of the same experiences. This book is a joyful, nostalgic read."
Ellen Dauplaise

Nurses' Caps and Angels' Wings

Nurses' Caps and Angels' Wings

A Glimpse of Student Life in the 1960s

Ruth Boettcher

Copyright 2014
Published by M&B Global Solutions Inc.
ISBN: 978-1-942731-08-5

Nurses' Caps and Angels' Wings

All rights reserved. No part of this book may be used or reproduced by any means, graphic, scanning, electronic, or mechanical, including photocopying, recording, taping or by any information storage retrieval system without the written permission of the publisher.

*This book is dedicated
to the graduating class of 1965.*

Contents

	Introduction	9
1.	Getting Used to the Big City	11
2.	We Were Never Alone	13
3.	Why Did You Go Into Nursing?	15
4.	I Begin Nursing School	17
5.	Physicals for the School of Nursing	25
6.	Breakfast Inspections	27
7.	Roommates and Friends	33
8.	Housemothers	39
9.	Last Name Only	45
10.	Rehtlaw Hospital	47
11.	Doctors Dating Nurses and Students	55
12.	Making Beds and Giving Injections	57
13.	Laundry Day	61
14.	Fantastic Food	65
15.	Maturing Quickly	71

16. Death and Autopsy 75

17. Autopsy 79

18. Capping, Choir Concerts and Chapel 83

19. Night Shift 87

20. Delivering Care 93

21. The Cab Driver 99

22. An Affair 103

23. Maybe Nursing Isn't For Me 109

24. Pediatric Affiliation and a Bathroom Secret 113

25. Jacksonville Psychiatric Affiliation 119

26. We Live in the Apartment 125

27. She's Married? 127

28. After Graduation 129

29. Angel Mechanic 133

30. Lila Enlists 139

31. Encounter with Eduardo 143

32. Epilogue 147

33. More From Ruth Boettcher 149

Nurses' Caps and Angels' Wings

Introduction

This is the story of my time as a nursing student in Chicago in the early 1960s. The names of individuals mentioned in this book have been changed to protect me, the innocent and the infamous. It is a story of what I did and how I felt during that time. I have tried to describe the experiences of daily life as a nursing student in the classroom and the dormitory, as well as the experiences of a student working in a hospital at that time.

The story will be interesting to my classmates and other nurses of our era as they remember how things were then. It will also be of interest to students in nursing school today as they compare yesterday's nursing with today's nursing. Other medical professionals, as well as readers who want to know how things were in the 1960s, will also find this interesting reading.

As I write this, it has been fifty years since I entered nursing school and nearly that since graduation. Much has changed in medicine during that time. Before memories of former times are lost, I thought it would be good to write about things I can remember as if they were yesterday.

I know you will enjoy getting a glimpse of how nursing was then. Some things were very different then, but some things remain the same. Today there are many new medications and advances in technology. However, nursing is still a challenging profession and the care of the patient is still the most important task.

Chapter 1

Getting Used to the Big City

The first day at nursing school, I was met by an upper class student who volunteered to be my "big sister." She gave me some good advice: "Don't go out of the dorm alone. Chicago is a big city and this is a changing neighborhood."

The neighborhood had been a bastion for wealthy people in the past. They were now retired and elderly. Polish immigrants had moved in to buy the houses that came up for sale, and now Puerto Ricans were buying the houses of the Polish immigrants, who were looking to better their lives by moving to the western suburbs. "It is not safe for a young girl to be out alone," she said.

That sounded a bit extreme to me, since I had a lot of freedom in the little town where I had lived before coming to Chicago. There I was able to walk everywhere alone with no fear.

The day after I arrived, it was reported that a young woman had been beaten up in the park across the street from the hospital by a gang of boys. Two days later, a patient jumped to her death in the middle of the night from a fourth floor window of the hospital. We saw the spot where she landed when we were on our way to breakfast in the hospital dining room the next morning. The body had been removed, but there was still a damp, red area on the sidewalk.

Someone being beaten up and someone jumping to their death were two incidents that would be quite shocking at any time, but to have them happen in the first few days I was in Chicago was even more terrifying. I tried to put the events out of my mind and concentrate on being a student nurse at Rehtlaw Memorial Hospital School of Nursing.

Chapter 2
We Were Never Alone

There was hardly ever a time when we were alone. We went everywhere in groups of at least two or four. We talked about everything with each other: nursing conditions, diagnoses, patients, classes. We discussed our lives, our families, our parents and boys. We did take our exams individually, of course, but everything else we did in groups. We went everywhere laughing and talking loudly.

It wasn't hard for me to do everything in groups, because I came from a large family at home. There was hardly a time even at home that I was by myself without some member of my family being with me. This student nursing life was just like an extension of my home life. There were some girls who had not come from large families. They did not always find doing things in groups to their liking. They were not used to moving in packs.

Nurses' Caps and Angels' Wings

Chapter 3

Why Did You Go Into Nursing?

When we were little, Mama would read to my brothers and me in our big dining room in the house in Iowa. There was very little furniture, but we had a massive wooden rocker with wide wooden arms. One of us would perch on the arm on one side of the chair and another would stake claim to the arm on the other side. The other two of us would snuggle in the chair on my mother's lap. My sister was usually asleep in the bassinet.

Mama read endlessly to us. "The Pokey Little Puppy" and "Babar Goes to the Circus" were just a few of the books she read. She also read us stories from a large Bible storybook she had. When she was done reading for the day, she would talk to us. She would talk to us about what we would be when we grew up. Her dearest wish was that the boys would be pastors. She wanted me to marry a pastor and she wanted me to be a teacher, a deaconess, a nurse and especially, a missionary. She wanted at least one of us to be a missionary.

We weren't allowed to talk back to our parents in those days or we would have been punished. So silently I said to myself, "Don't look at me, Mama. I don't want to be a missionary, and I definitely don't want to marry a pastor."

I knew I didn't want to be a teacher. I didn't have patience with my little brothers. So of the choices Mama was putting before me, being a nurse was the only choice that might even vaguely interest me.

Chapter 4

I Begin Nursing School

When I reached age 18, my choice, as I saw it, was still nursing school. There were two nursing schools that my parents and I had discussed. One was 75 miles from our home and the other one was in Chicago. By this time we had moved to Ohio and lived 250 miles from Chicago. My best friend and high school classmate, Jane, was applying to the school closest to our home. I wanted to go to that school to be close to my best friend. I wanted to make an application only to the school where Jane was going; but to please my parents, I began to make applications to both schools.

In December of our senior year in high school, our principal informed me that a $400 scholarship was available to a student who wanted to go into nursing. I applied for it. The scholarship could be used to pay tuition at the nursing school nearest my home. The nursing school in Chicago was offering a larger scholarship, but I really wanted to go to the nursing school to which my friend was applying.

When the $400 scholarship was awarded to me, I was very happy. Jane and I would be going to nursing school together. That day I was doing the family washing and had hung the clothes on the line to dry. My mother came out to the clothesline and began helping me take the dry clothes off the line, fold them, and put them in the basket.

"I really think you should go to the nursing school in Chicago," she said, "Even though you have been awarded the $400 scholarship to the nursing school close to our home, there will be an obligation connected with it. The obligation will be that you will be expected to come back and work at Allen Memorial Hospital here in our small town for at least a year after you graduate from nursing school. When you graduate from nursing school, I know you will not want to be tied to that obligation."

"I won't mind," I said.

"I think you will," she said. "Much will change in the three years you are in nursing school. When you graduate, you will be ready to spread your wings and move on to bigger things than our town has to offer."

I didn't understand what she was saying and didn't catch the real meaning of her words.

I thought she was just being controlling and trying to keep me from doing what I really wanted: going to the school where my best friend would be going. But, I did as I was told. I continued with the application to the school of nursing in Chicago.

The first thing I had to do was send for a copy of my birth certificate. "This is strange," I thought. "I am alive and I am me. Why would anyone doubt that I exist and require a birth certificate?"

I also had to take the National League of Nursing exam before completing the application. The result of that exam was required on the application form. I was granted an interview by the Rehtlaw School of Nursing in Chicago. The date was set for spring, but we had to change it because our high school choral contest fell on the same day. The school could have eliminated me from consideration when I requested a date change for my interview, but I didn't care because I really wanted to go to the other school of nursing anyway. They granted a date change. Finally, I went for the interview. It went well and I was accepted.

A physical exam with my family physician was required along with the necessary immunizations before I could enter Rehtlaw School of Nursing. My mother helped me schedule these, as well as plan what items of clothing I needed to add to my meager wardrobe before I left for Chicago. She also helped me plan what personal items I would need to buy before leaving home. I sewed the clothes I would need, using my mother's sewing machine in the dining room of our house. I sewed a pink wool suit, jacket, skirt, and a dressy blouse. I sewed another skirt and blouse for every day. I would not need many clothes, because we would be wearing student uniforms most of the time.

Most of the items I used at home were shared with my brothers and sister. It was nice to now have my own tube of toothpaste, mouthwash, and my own towels and washcloths to take with me. This was new for me. I really did not have much of what I could really call my own before this.

I remember arriving at the nurse's dormitory with one suitcase, a box which contained my raincoat, and an extra pair of walking shoes.

The upper class student who came to help me carry in my things and was assigned to be my "big sister" said, "Is this all you have?"

It was a suitcase that my father had newly purchased especially for me and it contained items that belonged only to me. I thought it was quite a lot.

"Most students can hardly carry in all their things," she said. "At least you won't have trouble fitting these things into the tiny closet in your room."

My father had driven me to Chicago that day, and two of my brothers were also in the car. We dropped off one of my brothers at a university about one hundred miles south of Chicago, and the other brother was on his way to a college in Milwaukee, Wisconsin. I was the in-between stop.

I had dragged my feet until the end because I still wanted to go to nursing school with my friend, Jane. However, my parents had the upper hand. I had no money and I was totally dependent on them for financial support. Was my mother really concerned that I would not want to be obligated to work in our small town hospital, or was she mainly concerned about the money they would have to pay for my tuition? They already had two boys in college, and now I was going away to school, too.

My father was a pastor and did not make a big salary, but even a father with a large salary would have found it a challenge to pay for three children in college at once. The scholarship to the Chicago school was much larger, so naturally that would have been a bigger consideration for my parents. The other school would have been a larger financial burden for them.

If I had wanted to go to the school closer to home, I would have had to find a way to pay for the fees on my own. If I had gone against their wishes, my parents would probably have disowned me and there would have been a different ending to this story. Instead, I did things their way. I was still financially dependent on them. I didn't see how I could foot the bill for the tuition myself. Most likely it was still a financial hardship for my parents, even though the scholarship was larger.

I was thinking only about what I wanted. I felt pushed, forced, ambivalent and angry, but I stuffed my emotions. That is what I usually had to do, since we were not allowed to talk back, ever. I really didn't know what else to do. The school of my choice would have been closer to them. I would have thought that they would have wanted me to be closer to them. I could have come home more often. I would have thought they would have wanted that, too. Chicago was farther away from home – a world away. They sent me there instead. I made do and tried to adjust.

They thought they were sending me to a Lutheran, Christian school. In some respects it was, but in other respects it was anything but Christian. I don't know if they ever knew just how far away from home and into another world they had sent me. Indeed, I would not be obligated to come back to our small town hospital to work for a year, but I would learn more about life and how to be strong in my faith than they realized. Both the way of life I knew and my faith would be sorely tested.

Nurses' Caps and Angels' Wings

Chapter 5

Physicals for the School of Nursing

One of the first weeks after entering nursing school, the students were told that an appointment had been made for each of us to have a physical.

"Why do we have to go for this physical?" I asked myself. "I just had a physical at home with my family physician in order to fulfill the requirements for entering this school of nursing."

The other first-year students and I were very busy studying and working on the floor, doing our clinical procedures by this time. We didn't relish the idea of having to undergo another physical, but we had no choice since this second physical seemed to be required by the school.

At the appointed time, each student had to go over to the hospital exam room set up for this purpose. Dr. Jones, the student health doctor, performed the physicals. He was also the chairman of the medical staff at Rehtlaw Memorial Hospital. Miss Munro, the nursing arts instructor, was present in the room when the physicals were performed. Each student was asked to disrobe and put on the ugly hospital gown to facilitate the exam. I had always been uncomfortable disrobing, putting on the hospital gown and having a physical done. But at home my doctor, who was a wonderful woman, made the experience a bit more pleasant. This exam just seemed unnecessary.

After the exam, I went back to class and continued the beginning of my life as a student nurse.

Chapter 6

Breakfast Inspections

The students were on probation for the first six months we were in nursing school. We mainly went to classes. These classes were conducted in the classroom on the first floor of the nurses' dormitory. There were also clinical procedures taught and then performed in the hospital, such as making beds, giving bed baths for bed-bound patients, passing medications and giving injections. Life was pretty much eat, sleep, work and study. Our world was the nurses' dorm and the hospital, across the street and just a half-block down.

We ate all meals in the hospital dining room. The girls usually walked en masse to the dining room for lunch after our morning classes and then went in smaller groups for the evening meal, which would be served as early as 4 p.m. We went in smaller groups for breakfast after getting up and ready for the day.

After six months of probation, the students who passed their finals and clinicals received their nursing caps at the capping ceremony. Up until that time, we had been working at the hospital in uniforms and without caps.

Now we came to breakfast in our uniforms. The uniform consisted of a short-sleeved, blue and white striped dress that was mid-calf length. It had a starched white collar and cuffs. This dress was worn with long white nurse's stockings and white nurse's shoes. I wore a size 10 shoe and was very self-conscious of how large my feet looked in those white shoes. Over the striped dress was a stiffly starched white pinafore apron. The girls tried to wear this apron two days in a row, but the first day we put the apron on it was starched so stiffly that it would hardly bend. How we were able to work in it at all was a marvel. Young people can make most anything work. Some of the girls complained about the uniform, but mostly they just put up with it. The last item of clothing, of course, was the white nurse's cap.

Miss Munro, the Nursing Arts instructor, came to breakfast every morning during the week. She sat at a table near the entrance to the dining room facing the door where the students entered. She appeared to be a little old lady in an absolutely immaculate white nurse's uniform. Actually, she was an instructor on a mission. Her mission was to inspect each student as she walked through the door to the dining room. Anyone who did not pass Miss Munro's inspection was sent back to the dorm to change.

One girl was sent back because she had a spot on her shoelace. Another girl was sent back because her white shoes were not polished, another because her apron appeared soiled. Most students spent a lot of time the evening before making sure their uniforms were spotless and complete. Students wasted valuable time going back to the dorm to change if Miss Munro found a spot on a uniform. A student might miss breakfast going back and changing, because everyone had to report for duty on the hospital floor at 7 o'clock sharp.

I was never sent back to the dorm for any deficiency in my uniform. But at the end of the grading period, Miss Munro still gave me a C+ in grooming. I was furious. I had all A's and B's but was given a C+ in grooming. I went to see Miss Munro to complain.

"Miss Boettcher," said Miss Munro peering over her glasses. "Your hair is flyaway and never seems to be combed."

I couldn't believe it. My hair was very short and only needed to be brushed straight in the morning before going out the door. The summer before my senior year, I had let my friend cut my hair. To my horror, the haircut left me with hair an inch long all over my head. The result was a pixie-like hairdo that was very short. It had just now grown out enough to brush in the morning. Understandably, I had not wanted to get another haircut before leaving home, but here it was a year and a bit later, and the hair was starting to grow out and look a bit unkempt. I was so busy with classes and clinicals that I had neglected to really give my hair a good look. Now I was away from my mother's hairdresser and had no money to get a proper cut. What could I do?

My roommate, Mary, had hair about the same length. She put her hair up in rollers every night. Mary had extra rollers and gave them to me to roll up my hair each night. That worked. Each morning I took the rollers out, brushed my hair into a neat style, and used hair spray to hold down any flyaway strands. That hair was guaranteed not to move even in a strong wind. The next grading period, I received an A in grooming from Miss Munro.

This began my quest for a hairdo that would not only pass Miss Munro's muster, but would look as good after an eight-hour shift as it had in the morning when the day began. As my hair got longer, I tried larger rollers until I achieved the hairdo called "the bubble," which was very popular then and had the Sandra Dee look. Eventually, it was long enough that I had to pin it up. I experimented with a French twist and the Beehive, both popular in the 1960s. Both of these hairdos required major back-combing and hair spraying. Sometimes these more extensive hairdos required up to an hour to complete. I had to get up earlier to get my hair done before breakfast. Mary continued to wear her hair short and curly.

Miss Munro also instructed the students in several other facets of our grooming. We were not to wear perfume, since it might nauseate the patient we were caring for. We were not to wear jewelry, because it was thought bacteria could be carried from our rings to the patient. Bracelets and necklaces would get in the way of care-giving.

We could not wear bright red nail polish, because it was considered to be in bad taste by Miss Munro. We could, however, wear clear nail polish or light colors such as white pearl, and light coral and pink.

Chapter 7

Roommates and Friends

Our class was divided into groups of six students each for study purposes and clinical groups. Roommates were assigned by alphabetical order. My roommate, Millie, fancied herself to be an expert on everything, including all things hip and cool: cool clothes, cool shoes, cool coats. In her opinion, I had none of the above.

She smoked. I didn't, which to her meant that I was not part of the "in" crowd. Even though she had gone to another nursing school and was now starting over at this school of nursing, Millie thought she knew everything.

In a matter of weeks, she had had enough of me and began giving me the silent treatment. After she hadn't talked to me for several days, I couldn't stand it any longer. I ran weeping to the housemother and asked for a change of roommates. Mrs. Asher, a chain-smoker herself, told me it would be impossible to get another roommate just because Millie smoked. All the rooms in the dorm were filled to capacity with two girls to a room. She assured me that no one else wanted to change roommates. I went back to my room sobbing. Millie pretended she had no idea why I was crying.

The next day I was notified that a student had quit. No reason was given. Now her bed was vacant, but it was on the second floor with the S group. Her roommate, Gillian, agreed to my becoming her new roommate. Gillian was a strange girl. She kept to herself most of the time, but she was friendly. Even with her strange ways, she was not egotistical or condescending. Her mother and her sister visited her often and she introduced them to me. She was from Chicago.

Gillian was in a different clinical group, so we didn't work or study together and we didn't see each other often. I was in the A and B group and she was in the S group. We didn't see each other unless all the first-year students were in class together. Then we were always seated in alphabetical order, so we weren't even seated close together. We became roommates in late September or early October. By early

November, I knew why Gillian kept to herself. She was not doing well in her course work. I was striving to get A's and B's and studying hard, but Gillian was having difficulty just keeping up. I didn't ask Gillian specifically about her grades and she never told me, so I was surprised when she didn't return after the Thanksgiving holiday break. No explanation was given; the housemother just told me that Gillian would not be back. We hadn't even exchanged addresses and phone numbers, so I couldn't call her to find out how she was doing and if she was all right. I suddenly had a private room, and I was not used to being alone.

After the Thanksgiving break it was cold, with subzero temperatures in Chicago. We were going to classes, studying long hours, and going to the hospital every day to do our clinical work. The off hours were very few. We didn't get a lot of sleep and we lived in very close quarters. Suddenly, there was yelling at the other end of the hall. Mary was being yelled at by her roommate, Silvia.

Silvia, a very pretty girl, was hogging the bathroom, not allowing others time to have a relaxing shower after work. Mary finally went down to complain to the housemother. Other girls were berating Mary for being a snitch. Mary was beside herself and in tears. I went and sat with Mary in her room and talked to her. I agreed with her and told her she had done the right thing. Eventually everyone cooled down, the sobbing subsided and we all went back to our rooms for the night.

Shortly after this big blow-up, a single room across the hall from Mary and Silvia's room became vacant when the upper class person who had been living there went out of the city for her psychiatric clinical training. Silvia took the single room, which left Mary without a roommate. Mary approached me and offered me the opportunity to be her roommate.

"Let me think about this," I said, just a little wary, since this would be my third roommate in a very short time. In my mind, I was wondering if moving in with her would be such a great idea because of the loud squabble I had witnessed between Mary and Silvia.

Finally I told Mary, "Let's try being roommates for a week. If we can get along, we'll make it official and become roommates. If it doesn't work, I'll move back to my own room."

I must admit I had more than a little trepidation the first night of our trial week, but things went well and we found we had much in common. I was a pastor's daughter and she was a teacher's daughter. Both of us grew up in large families and in homes that were financially strapped. Mary usually had to have things her way. I went along with what she wanted unless it was something with which I just could not agree. Then I spoke up and Mary usually listened. We usually were able to work out our differences. Mary was from Chicago and I was from a small town. I thought she usually knew more than I did – at least about how things were done in Chicago.

Mary had become good friends with the two girls in the next room: Lila and Victoria. They quickly included me and we became "The Gang of Four." It was a good gang – safety in numbers, and for our own good as well the good of others.

Victoria, Lila and I were pastors' daughters and Mary was a teacher's daughter. We had all lived in the spotlight of the parish life as kids and our fathers all had the very low salaries of church workers. We were all part of large families. Coming from financially poor backgrounds and living with parents who expected perfect behavior and excellent grades, we had a lot in common. We became fast friends off duty as well as on duty, helping each other when we worked together in the hospital.

This camaraderie was to carry over into our adulthood after graduation. We remained the best of friends even when there were long stretches when we didn't see each other or talk to one another. The bond formed under such intense studying and clinical work, coupled with such similar backgrounds, was unbelievably strong and unbreakable.

Chapter 8

Housemothers

The nurses' residence was a half-block down the street from the hospital. It was a typical Chicago brownstone apartment building and had three floors. It usually was locked. However, the front door was unlocked during the day when the housemother sat at her desk. The front door led into a vestibule to the right, which had a sliding glass window where one of the housemothers sat and functioned as a receptionist. One of the housemothers was always there to answer the switchboard, observe the students as they came and went, screen visitors, and monitor the doors. Visitors could not get past the housemother because a second door, inside the vestibule, was locked. Each student had her own key to open the second door, as well as a key to her dorm room, but any visitor had to speak to the housemother to be allowed through the second door and enter the nurses' residence.

The outside door was locked at 10 p.m. Curfew was at 10 p.m. The students had to be in by that time because "lights out" was at 10 p.m. If a student was not going to be in until the last minute, special permission had to be obtained ahead of time from the housemother. Once a month, each student was allowed to stay out until 11 p.m. This was called a "late night" and special permission for this privilege had to be obtained in advance from the housemother.

Since there were no cell phones at that time, students had to sign out when they left and in when they returned. The housemothers were responsible for about 75 students. There were no male students enrolled at that time. The housemothers had to know where each student was at all times.

If parents telephoned a student, the housemother needed to know where to reach the student. If the student made a medication error that was discovered after she had left the hospital, the housemothers needed to know where to reach the student so they could return to the hospital and rectify the error. If the student left the hospital with part of her assignment left undone, the hospital called the housemother, who called the student to come back to the hospital.

Students were to be in their beds with lights out at 10 p.m. on the dot. The student's room door had to be locked. Then the housemother would come around to each room, turn her key in the lock, open the door of the student's room, check by the hallway light that the student was in bed, close the door, and lock it by turning her key again. None of the doors locked automatically, so the key had to be used each time.

Many times, I waited until the housemother had left the floor and then turned on the light to read again or study. Not a lot of late night activity went on during the week because all students had to be on duty by 7 a.m. or at class by 8 a.m. Students also worked most weekends, having only one weekend off per month. Everyone was pretty tired after an eight-hour shift, so there was usually no problem with 10 o'clock lights out.

The nurses' residence was located on an alley, and there was a locked back door and a locked gate. It was rumored that some upper class students had let themselves out of the back gate. To do this, a student needed an accomplice to let her back into the dorm, because no student had a key to the back gate or the back door.

There were three housemothers: Mrs. Asher, Mrs. Engler and Mrs. Coleman. Most of the students were between the ages of 17 and 21. To the students, Mrs. Coleman seemed like she was at least 100 years old. Mrs. Asher and Mrs. Engler seemed to be at least 80. In any case, they seemed ancient. Most likely they were all in their fifties or sixties.

Mrs. Coleman usually was on at night and made the bed checks. She had a wrinkled face, but was always smiling and very pleasant. She was always well dressed, with never a hair out of place. She was short and stooped. She was probably 4-foot-11 if she was an inch. It must have been very difficult for her to reach the locks on the room doors, because the lock was several inches above the doorknob. In any case, nothing ever got past her.

Mrs. Asher seemed to be the one in charge, but the students never actually were told about the hierarchy of the housemothers. The students just went about their schedules, signing in and out as they came and went, passing the housemother on duty at the desk and the switchboard behind the sliding glass window.

Mrs. Engler was more likely to be on days. She was friendly and the students thought she was a pushover. She never seemed to know what day it was. Toward the end of her time there, I thought I detected Mrs. Engler slurring some of her words when she spoke. It was whispered that she had an alcohol problem.

I had already seen many things in my time as a student nurse. The students went about their business and let the housemothers do their thing. The students were wise beyond their years by this time and were used to caring for sick people. They cared for their housemother, too, by continuing to be respectful to her.

Nurses' Caps and Angels' Wings

Chapter 9

Last Name Only

We were never to divulge our first name to patients while we were on duty. So I was always addressed as Miss Boettcher, Mary was always Miss Rhodes, Lila was always Miss Lincoln, and Victoria was always Miss Nunes.

This form of address was to preserve our professionalism and keep us from getting too familiar with our patients. We were to address our patients also as Miss, Mrs. or Mr., and use only their last names. The nursing instructors, head nurses and doctors also were never addressed by their first names.

In a way, this formality backfired from its original purpose of keeping us from getting too familiar with patients and fellow nurses. Our last names quickly became our nicknames. So forever after I was always simply "Boettcher" to my classmates and to people who knew me well. My friends were always "Rhodes," "Lincoln," and "Nunes."

Even after we were married and took our married names, and were living far apart from each other, we still fell back into calling each other by our last names, which had now become our nicknames for each other.

Chapter 10

Rehtlaw Hospital

The hospital was an imposing red brick structure taking up two entire city blocks. It actually looked like a large office building, but it was in a residential neighborhood. It wasn't until the hospital was remodeled in 1963, and a canopy with a circle drive under it was added to the front of the building, that the structure began to look more like a hospital. The hospital was like a little city within itself, with a dining room and kitchen, laboratory, administrative offices, physician rooms, pharmacy, patient floors and nurses' stations.

On the first floor were the hospital kitchen and dining room, administrative offices, morgue, lab, lobby and reception area. Second floor was the orthopedic floor and laundry. Third floor was the medical floor and the chapel. Fourth floor was the post-surgical floor.

Fifth floor was obstetrics and the nursery, and the sixth floor held the operating suites.

There were 50 beds on each of the orthopedics, medical and post-surgical floors. Each floor had two private rooms. The orthopedics and post-surgical floors each had an eight-bed men's ward. Obstetrics had a four-bed women's ward. Third floor, the medical floor, had a four-bed pediatric ward.

None of the rooms had private bathrooms. Those patients who were able were obliged to use the common bathroom and shower room at the end of the long hallway. Those who could not walk to the bathroom had to use bedpans. Part of the training of a student nurse was learning how to properly administer a bedpan.

Each bedpan had a striped denim cover. This cover was to be placed on the bedpan as it was carried from the patient's room to the utility room to be emptied into the hopper. The cover was also to be placed back on the bedpan when it was carried back to the patient's room. All of this was done without the aid of disposable gloves. Think of the number of steps the nurses made in an eight-hour shift just carrying bedpans!

Student nurses also gave bed baths to those patients who could not walk to the shower at the end of the hallway. There were no sinks in the rooms, so if a patient needed a bed bath, we had to carry water from the utility room in a basin. Then, of course, we had to carry the water back to the utility room to be dumped after completing the bath. More steps again. The number of steps made in getting water for the bed bath, together with the number of steps made in carrying bedpans, was phenomenal and made for some pretty tired student nurses.

Of course, the hospital was open 24 hours a day, seven days a week, 365 days a year, so continuous staffing was necessary. In the 1960s, students played a large part in filling the staffing needs of the hospital. When we were supervised by a clinical instructor, we might be assigned two or three patients; but when we worked on Saturdays and Sundays, there was no clinical instructor and we would be assigned more patients for care and bathing.

One particularly busy Saturday, Mary and I were working on the medical floor. Each of us was assigned 10 patients. We learned to work quickly and efficiently, and did enormous amounts of work in a short period of time. We learned to work together to help each other with patients who couldn't turn themselves as we gave them baths or made their beds.

Working on the floors in the winter was one thing, because the hospital had a good boiler and heating system. However, the summer was a different matter. There was no air conditioning except on the obstetrics floor and in surgery. Working on the floors in the heat of summer, especially fourth floor, was grueling. We would come off an eight-hour shift with uniforms wringing wet. Surviving in the heat of the Chicago summers was a superhuman feat. We were young and the heat didn't bother us as much as it would an older person. Air conditioning was just coming into vogue and was not yet a requirement in hospitals. The students and patients had to put up with the conditions as they were.

Until 1963, when the new addition was built onto Rehtlaw Hospital, there was no piped-in oxygen. Patients needing oxygen were placed in oxygen tents. It was really a challenge for the students to take care of a patient in an oxygen tent. There were zippers on the sides of the tents with flaps we could open if we needed to give medication to the patient. If we needed to fluff the pillows or make the bed with the patient in it, we had to stick our head into the tent. The nurse's cap always got in the way when we put our head into the tent or took it out. Nursing caps were professional looking, but often a nuisance. The tents were hooked up to oxygen tanks to keep the supply of oxygen flowing. The tanks were almost as tall as the students themselves. We had to go down to the oxygen storage room, wrestle the tanks onto a dolly with wheels, and take the tank back up the service elevator to the patient's room.

The oxygen delivered inside the tent was not always as high a concentration as the patient needed. The students were all aghast when the husband of one of our favorite instructors died of pneumonia after being in an oxygen tent for several days. Things improved once patients began to receive oxygen via oxygen mask and nasal cannula, and they could receive the concentration of oxygen they needed.

Blood was administered from glass bottles at Rehtlaw Hospital in the very early 1960s. Nurses went to the blood bank in the hospital lab to obtain units that would be given intravenously to the patient. Everything was always done quickly and the staff was always in a hurry. One of the students in my group was sent to the lab to get a pint of blood that was waiting there for a patient. In her hurry to get back to the floor to get the IV started, she tripped and dropped the bottle. What a mess that was. It was really an improvement when blood was finally packaged in plastic containers. At least then there was no chance of breaking a glass bottle.

The elevators were not automatic like the ones we know today. The students were able to operate them, but sometimes there was a problem of getting the floor of the elevator to line up with the floor we wanted to get out on. Most days there was an elevator operator to help with that. He was a wizened little old man who wore an official beige poplin jacket and smiled at us when we got on and off the elevator. He knew all the students by name and was very kind to us. He was especially helpful when a patient who had died needed to be transported directly to the morgue. He fixed the elevator so it would not stop at any floors other than the floor the morgue was on. That way the elevator door wouldn't open and give an unsuspecting visitor a scare.

The phones also were not automatic and needed an operator. The person for that job had to work as fast as lightning. The operator often connected the nurses' dorm with the hospital and vice versa. The operator working when I first came to Rehtlaw Hospital was so jumpy from working so many years at the switchboard that she disconnected calls as often as she connected them. Most often, a caller had to make two or three attempts before a call finally went through.

Chapter 11

Doctors Dating Nurses and Students

Some things that went on at the hospital were surprising and even shocking to first-year students. It was rumored that Dr. Jones was seeing one of the young single head nurses. Everyone knew Dr. Jones was married. When Dr. Jones' wife got cancer, she was admitted to a private room in Rehtlaw Hospital on the floor where that nurse worked. Everyone thought it was outrageous.

The first-year students had many other things on their minds. We had to study, function well, go on duty and take care of our patients. We had to clear our minds of these shocking things and concentrate on the work at hand. We had to put this outrageous situation out of our minds in order to do our work properly, but it was disturbing, especially to me.

"How does everyone except Dr. Jones' wife know that he is dating this single nurse?" I wondered to myself. "How can that nurse function while caring for Dr. Jones' wife?"

These were questions that went through my mind. I thought the situation was outrageous, but there was nothing I could do about it. It seemed that it was an accepted practice for a doctor to date anyone he pleased. Everyone knew about it but no one did anything about it, just whispered about it.

One student nurse in the dorm was seeing another married doctor. She came back to the dorm one night wearing a fur jacket he had given her. On another occasion, he had given her jewelry. What was the most frustrating to me was that so many people did not respect marriage or keep their marriage vows.

Chapter 12

Making Beds and Giving Injections

Making beds was the first big nursing procedure we learned. We were oriented to the linen room and the utility room. We were shown how to assemble the fresh linens we would need to make the beds, put on clean pillowcases, and replace the towel and washcloth for the patients we were assigned to that day. The utility room was where we took the soiled sheets and towels to throw them down the laundry chute. We quickly learned to assemble packets of clean linens and take them around to all the rooms of the patients assigned to us. It saved time if we did that before starting with the first patient.

We learned to make a bed by starting from one side of the bed and then going to the other side to finish. The sheets and bedspreads were pre-folded in the laundry so that we could accomplish this "one side first" method of making the bed. By using this method, it was possible to make the bed with the patient in it. This was very efficient, especially if the patient was on bed rest or in traction.

Making the bed totally from one side and then going to the other side to finish saved many steps. Going back and forth from one side of the bed to the other would have exhausted us by the time we finished our last patient. Our assignments increased from one or two patients each day to five patients each day. On the weekends, we could be caring for as many as 10 patients.

The next big thing we learned was how to give injections. I gave my first injection with the nursing instructor present to ensure I was doing it the right way. If it wasn't enough to be nervous about giving an injection, there was the added stress of having the nursing instructor peering over my shoulder as I accomplished the procedure. It didn't help much that I was an 18-year-old young woman and that the patient was a middle-aged man.

The instructor watched me draw up the medication in the syringe in the medication room in the nurses' station. I placed the syringe and the card printed with the patient's name, the room number, the name of the medication, and the time it was to be given on a small tray, which I carried to the patient's room. The nursing instructor walked alongside me to the patient's room.

After checking the patient's wristband to verify his name and room number, I told the patient I was going to give the injection and then proceeded to do so. I was shocked and relieved that the patient seemed perfectly fine after the medication had been injected and I had removed the needle. I thanked the patient and exited the room.

"You did very well, Miss Boettcher," the nursing instructor said outside the room.

I barely heard her as I leaned against the wall and slid to the floor before I could faint.

"I think it is time for the students to go to the dining room for a break," the instructor announced.

Chapter 13

Laundry Day

You are probably wondering how the students kept their uniforms and aprons clean, stiff and starched. It was all done for them in the hospital laundry. The laundry was on the second floor of the hospital at the end of a long hallway on the orthopedic floor.

Each week, the students made their way back to the laundry to pick up their freshly starched and laundered uniforms for the upcoming week. Every student had her own laundry cubicle with her name on it in big black letters. These square wooden cubicles were against the back wall of the laundry. They were actually wooden shelves portioned into square bins so that each student had a cubbyhole that held her clean uniforms for the week. The bin was large enough to also hold clean sheets, and towels and washcloths for the week, and sometimes clean blankets.

A striped denim laundry bag had been issued to each student when they received their uniforms upon entering nursing school. Worn uniforms were placed into the laundry bag each day, and dirty sheets and towels were added to the bag. We deposited the bag full of dirty laundry in the designated cart when we made our way back to the laundry each week to pick up our clean uniforms and sheets.

These trips to the laundry again were usually not made alone. There were always four or five students who went together. They grabbed their laundry bags filled with a week's worth of soiled laundry and headed over to the hospital laundry, laughing boisterously and talking loudly all the way. I'm sure the patients on the orthopedic floor wondered what was going on as they passed the patients' rooms on the way to the laundry.

The queen of the laundry, the lady in charge, was Mrs. Luking. She always met the students as they came into the laundry area. When we opened the door of the laundry, a blast of warm air always hit our faces. There were always several pressing machines hissing as workers pressed the sheets that were to be put on the patient's beds, as well as the dorm beds of the students. Mrs. Luking was always pleasant enough, but she was a perfectionist. She met the students wearing her pink uniform starched and pressed within an inch of its life. She always had a delicate white nylon embroidered handkerchief peeking out of the breast pocket of her uniform. The embroidery was pink to match her uniform. Her lipstick was pink also, and her makeup was done to perfection. Her pink powdered makeup and blush completed the ensemble. She was kind, but always very professional. Nothing got past her and she always seemed to take her job too seriously.

The students were to tell Mrs. Luking if they had any problem stains or tears on their uniforms, if there were any missing buttons, or if they did not receive the right number of uniforms to last them for the coming week. Mrs. Luking, in turn, stopped a student to tell her that she had not turned in the correct number of uniforms the week before or that the student had failed to pick up her clean laundry. Nothing escaped the notice of Mrs. Luking. It was whispered that she had been a sergeant in the army.

She knew all of the students, and knew them by name – last name, of course. The student's names were written in black indelible ink on the inside yoke of each uniform, and on the inside of the back tie of each pinafore apron.

Chapter 14

Fantastic Food

I really liked the food served in the dining room. There were so many wonderful main dishes and interesting desserts. It was hard for me to believe all this delicious food even existed. At home, my mother served mostly simple meals of meat and potatoes and canned vegetables. She simply roasted chicken and beef in the oven. For our large family, my mother served vegetables she had raised in the garden and then canned for the winter. Desserts were fruits she also had canned.

Mr. Chaus was the chef at the hospital. He was from France. He was short and had thinning hair covered with a tall white chef's hat, which he wore while supervising the serving in the hospital dining room. He wore a starched white chef's jacket with white knotted cloth buttons. He was slightly stooped and shuffled when he walked. It was rumored that he had had syphilis, which caused his shuffling gait. One never knew what to believe about these rumors, but he would have had to have been totally cured of this disease to have been allowed to be the head chef and serve food for a hospital. We put the rumors out of their minds and enjoyed the food that was offered in the hospital dining room.

Mr. Chaus was in charge of the dining room, which served meals to the hospital employees, the medical staff of staff doctors and house residents, the nursing staff and the nursing students. He was also in charge of producing the meals served to the patients. A dietitian planned meals for patients needing special diets, such as cardiac patients, diabetics and surgical patients and others who had specific dietary needs, but Mr. Chaus and his staff produced the meals.

In spite of the rumors floating around about Mr. Chaus, none of the students ever got sick from the food. I especially liked the huge pork chops stuffed with delicious bread stuffing, along with mounds of creamy mashed potatoes. The extra-large French-fried shrimp melted in my mouth. I had never tasted shrimp or shrimp sauce before I came to the Rehtlaw Hospital dining room, nor had I tasted stuffed pork chops for that matter. Mr. Chaus also made great liver and onions, which were as good as those my mother made at home.

The salads were delicious. My mother could not afford to serve salad for our large family at home, so I really enjoyed the fresh salad in the dining room. Mr. Chaus' Waldorf salad was especially good. I had not had Waldorf salad at home, either.

All the foods, except for the salads, were served piping hot. As the students took their trays and went through the serving line, we passed the giant coffee maker. I didn't drink coffee, but I always liked the smell of the coffee perking. On a cool fall or winter day, the smell of hot steaming coffee added to the wonderful atmosphere of the dining room.

The students sat together at one table. The head nurses sat together at another table, and the doctors and residents sat at another table. The students were always thrilled when the doctors and residents passed by their table and said, "Hi girls."

All the students shouted their hellos, waved and giggled. There was a lot of loud talking and laughing, and there was quite a sense of community in the hospital dining room. It was loud and crowded, but it was nice and everyone liked the atmosphere.

Later, the hospital addition included a new steel and glass modern dining room. The students felt that the new dining room just did not have the charm that the old crowded, wood-trimmed dining room had.

As for desserts, I loved the ice cream served on Sundays. Often on Sundays, dessert featured coffee ice cream with rum raisin sauce. Another favorite was peppermint ice cream with actual bits of peppermint candy mixed in the ice cream. The staff served both kinds of ice cream in dainty, fluted glass dishes on a dessert plate, on which a lacy paper doily had been placed. On one side of the plate, next to the dainty little dish, was a coconut macaroon, freshly baked from Mr. Chaus' kitchen.

The students were not allowed to enter the dining room in slacks or shorts. Those were the days when one always dressed up when one went out. So even on Saturday and Sunday, the students had to change into a skirt or dress to go to the dining room for breakfast, lunch and dinner. The students thought this rule was ridiculous, but we were hungry and had to eat. And one never knew if Miss Munro would show up in the dining room unexpectedly.

But the students took matters into their own hands on weekends. Most weekends we worked and were wearing our uniforms anyway. But on the weekends we had off, we found a way to bend the rules: we wore shorts or slacks with the legs rolled up and put trench coats over these casual outfits to hide the fact that we were not wearing skirts.

The dining room opened at four o'clock in the afternoon, so the students went right when the dining room opened to avoid any chance of meeting Miss Munro. Our plan did not work as well in the summer. If it was 90 degrees, wearing a trench coat over our outfits was a bit uncomfortable, since there was no air-conditioning in the dining room.

Chapter 15

Maturing Quickly

Surgical techniques in the 1960s were not as refined as they are now. In caring for post-surgical patients, the students saw many long incisions and some gaping wounds. Incisions that were sutured and closed well were done by the best surgeons. The patients of the best surgeons came through the surgeries with less pain and the incisions were likely to heal faster.

There were some things the students saw that were difficult for them, as well as for the patients who experienced them. The colostomy surgery was one that was very difficult for the patient. Many patients saw it as the end of their life as they knew it. Helping the patient deal with the physical care of the colostomy was difficult enough, but helping them deal with the psychological aspect of a colostomy was sometimes more difficult. The patients were in physical discomfort and pain, but the psychological pain was devastating for many.

It was hard for the students to witness this psychological pain. The students matured quickly watching the outcome of this surgical procedure, caring for the patients and helping them begin to care for themselves.

The mastectomy was another procedure that was shocking for me. The first mastectomy patient that I cared for not only had her breast removed, but had muscle tissue from the underarm and chest wall also removed, leaving the patient with a lot of pain. She was psychologically devastated. It was one of the most shocking things I saw during my three years of nursing school.

Another patient who was a shock to me was one who had severe cirrhosis of the liver. A heavy drinker, he went into delirium tremens – or DTs – when he came into the hospital. He went into uncontrollable shaking and cried, telling the nurses that he saw insects crawling on his sheets. Of course, they weren't there. He told the nurses and doctors that he was driving down the highway in his bed and he didn't have any breaks or steering wheel. In his confused state, he was experiencing horrible crashes with his "vehicle." It was hard for the student nurses to see him suffer.

Another patient had a very severe abdominal wound. He had been shot by police in a robbery attempt. Sometimes the police were at his bedside. Sometimes he was just handcuffed to the side rails of the bed. The man was too weak to get up, but he was not too weak to swear. He swore at the students when they cared for his terrible abdominal wound and when they changed his dressings. He swore at the nurses when they entered the room and continued his tirade the whole time they were there. He was the worst patient that I had to deal with in all my years of nursing, even after graduation.

Experiencing these horrible cases, I continued to question whether nursing was really what I wanted to do for the rest of my life. The problem was that I didn't know what else I wanted to do instead. I knew I didn't want to go back home. I felt it was better for me to keep on with what I was doing until I had a clearer picture in my head of what I really wanted to do.

Nurses' Caps and Angels' Wings

Chapter 16

Death and Autopsy

The students spent many hours working in the hospital. During the weekdays, a nursing instructor would supervise our work. If there were interesting patient cases, the instructors wanted the students to observe that patient in order to have the experience of as many different case-diagnoses as possible.

One day, the instructor assigned me to a patient who was near death. The instructor talked with me about the patient and prepared me for the possibility that the patient could die while I was caring for him. The patient was comatose and not responding, but he was breathing. The family was at the bedside. They were extremely solemn and very concerned, knowing that the patient's condition was very serious.

I cared for the patient, giving a bed bath and making the bed with the patient in the bed as I had been taught to do. As soon as I had finished with the morning nursing cares, the patient began very labored breathing. There was a long pause after each breath until finally the patient took his last breath. It was hard for me to believe that the patient I had just been caring for had actually died. It was quite upsetting, even though the instructor had tried to prepare me for this moment. It was the first time I had been present at the time of a death. Witnessing the death had a profound impact on me. Seeing the patient take his last breath changed me forever. The patient was just gone. There was no life; it was such a loss.

This is when I realized how horrible and empty and lonely it is for the person who does not believe in eternal life. What comfort there is for the person who believes that God takes our loved ones to heaven immediately so that they can live with Him in eternal bliss and glory forever.

Seeing the patient take his last breath had a profound effect on me. I matured considerably in that moment. That weekend, I went to stay with my friend in the dorm at the teacher's college, where my friend was a student. My friend was obsessing over what to wear to dinner.

"You are worried about what to wear," I thought to myself. "What does it matter? I have seen a human being die. Stressing over what you will wear to dinner doesn't seem very important compared to that."

I felt like I had instantly become an adult, and it felt lonely. I wondered if I would ever again have common ground with my friend, who suddenly seemed like a child.

Chapter 17
Autopsy

The instructors tried hard to give the students experience in every kind of case they might encounter in their nursing career. One day, I was told to report to the morgue to observe an autopsy the pathologist would be doing that morning.

The morgue was a small, windowless room. It became almost stifling for me and the other students who were there to observe the autopsy. The pathologist, Dr. Kleinman, was a large, heavy-set man with a thick Eastern European accent. He was in the morgue preparing to begin the autopsy. He was wearing a black rubber apron over his clothes, but he was not wearing a shirt. I thought that was a bit odd, but the students had been cautioned never to question a doctor, so I tried to ignore it.

The body of the deceased person was laid out on a stainless steel autopsy table. Several students watched as the pathologist opened the skull. When the skull had been examined, the pathologist moved to examine the chest cavity. Finally, the abdominal cavity was examined. The deceased patient had died of cirrhosis of the liver, but the lungs were also diseased. They were black, indicating that the man had been a smoker as well as a drinker.

After the autopsy had been completed, the students began to leave. It had been difficult to look at the lifeless body, but it had been even more difficult to watch the body cavities being opened and examined, and the organs actually being weighed on a scale.

But Dr. Kleinman did not allow us to leave. He wanted us to observe a second autopsy. This time the body was that of an infant. That was even harder to watch. The baby had been born without a face and without a brain. The doctor taught as he worked. He said that many times when an infant is born with a major defect, there are sometimes one or two more defects that will mercifully not allow the child to live, thus sparing the child and the family from an impossible life situation.

Thankfully, after that case, we were allowed to leave for lunch. What was for lunch that day? You guessed it – liver and onions. None of us had much of an appetite.

Chapter 18
Capping, Choir Concerts and Chapel

The first six months in nursing school were the testing period. The first-year students were on probation and referred to as "probies." If they passed their exams, they made the grade and were invited to participate in the capping ceremony.

The capping ceremony was held at Mt. Horeb Lutheran church about 20 blocks from the hospital. The school of nursing rented a large bus to take all the students to the church together. We all wore our uniforms and were given navy blue woolen capes to wear over them to guard against the cold, night air. The upper class students wore their uniforms as well as their white starched caps. The first-year students wore only their uniforms and capes.

There was a beautiful candlelight service. At the end of the service, each first-year student was given a Florence Nightingale lamp with a candle in it. We recited the Florence Nightingale pledge, and then the director of nursing, with much pomp, placed a white starched cap on the head of each of the first-year students who had passed all their exams.

I was so happy. We were no longer "probies." We had made the grade. We were full-fledged student nurses.

Family and friends were invited to the capping ceremony, but my mother and father were unable to be there. Mary's parents and her sisters were there. They lived close enough that they could attend the ceremony and the reception afterwards.

We were taken back to the dorm again on the bus, singing all the way. We were all members of the Rehtlaw School of Nursing Choir. The director of this choir was Mr. Bloom. He was a music teacher who came every Wednesday after chapel to direct the student choir. Some of the songs sung on the bus were the sacred selections from choir practice, but some of the songs were ribald student nursing songs that were unofficially part of the tradition of the school of nursing. These songs were passed down from class to class. The students lived in a world in which the ribald coexisted with the sublime and sacred. We were young enough to believe we could have one foot in both worlds.

The student choir sang at student nurse gatherings and meetings, sometimes in chapel, and several times a year at a concert hall in downtown Chicago. For the concert, the students again rode downtown on the bus and filed into the concert hall. I was in awe when I saw the concert hall for the first time. It was beautiful and ornate and very old. It was grander than anything I had ever seen. The choir director assembled the students on stage and the concert began. Our voices sounded so beautiful in this grand concert hall, where the acoustics were designed to make every performance sound amazing. These concerts usually were given as fundraisers for the school of nursing.

Every Wednesday, Chapel services were held in the hospital chapel on the third floor of the hospital. The pastor at Mt. Horeb Lutheran Church officiated at these services. The services were designed for nurses who would be working on Sunday and would not be able to attend church. The pastor was very kind and fatherly. His services were a comfort in the midst of all the life-changing events I was experiencing as the months of nursing school progressed. The chapel services reminded me of home and family, bringing me back each week to the faith and values I had learned at home.

Chapter 19

Night Shift

Once the capping ceremony was over, we began wearing our caps whenever we were on duty. Then we began to work weekends. We worked the day shift on Saturdays and Sundays three weekends a month. During the week, we worked in the hospital from 7 am until 11 am. We took a break for lunch and then went to classes in the afternoon.

Beginning with our third year, we began to work the 3 pm – 11 pm shift. The hospital staffed the evening and night shifts with students, and the students were often the charge nurses on those evening shifts. There was a nursing supervisor who made rounds, and the students could call her if they needed advice on anything. Soon, we were also assigned the night shift, which was 11 pm – 7 am. When students first worked the night shift, a clinical instructor would be there at the early part of the shift to check that things were going all right.

On my first night shift, the clinical instructor, Miss King, walked through the unit where I was working. We talked over my assignment, and then I walked with her to the elevator on my way to taking care of a patient. As Miss King was standing in the elevator waiting for the door to close, she said, "Remember, Miss Boettcher, people die at night."

What a chilling statement for an instructor to make to a student who was just learning to work the night shift; a student who was already scared stiff about what could happen at night.

Miss King was often particularly sarcastic. She taught neurology and was the clinical instructor on the medical floor. During one of my neurology classes, Miss King was called away. When she returned, she announced to the students in a very subdued tone that President John F. Kennedy had been shot. Our instructor's voice then took on a respectful tone, quite different from that of her usual sarcasm, as she continued our study of the brain and its anatomy. She respectfully pointed out the path of the bullet and what happens to a brain and a body when struck by a bullet. We all held out hope that the president would recover, but Miss King knew instantly that it was not to be.

One of the patients I cared for that night was in very critical condition and was being given the drug Levophed intravenously. It is a very strong medication that regulates blood pressure. The medication drip in those days was controlled only by the roller clamp on the intravenous line. The sophisticated, computerized intravenous pumps were not yet available at Rehtlaw Hospital, and the roller clamp on the intravenous line was the only thing the nurses had to regulate the speed at which the medication was given to the patient.

Since I also had other patients, I would return to the first patient's room every fifteen minutes to count the drops being delivered to the patient through the intravenous line. I would slow down or speed up the prescribed number of drops per minute using the roller clamp. I did my best throughout the night shift to regulate the rate of medication delivery.

At the end of the night shift, I went back to the dorm to grab a nap and then went to the dining room for lunch. The nurses from the day shift relayed the news to me that the patient had died. They assured me the patient's death was not my fault, and that even perfect regulation of the medication would not have saved the patient's life. It was several days before I was convinced that the death was not my fault.

After that experience, I vowed always to do my utmost in every case, for every patient I cared for. I pledged always to give the very best care possible so that I would know that if something happened to the patient, it was not my fault. I kept that vow until I retired from nursing, giving care that I felt went above and beyond what was expected of any nurse. I could go home and sleep at night knowing that nothing bad would occur because of anything I failed to do. Consequently, I earned a reputation for being a good nurse who gave excellent care to all my patients.

Patients did die, however, and it fell to the nurse and nurse's aides on that shift to prepare the body to take to the morgue. One night, the nurse's aides and I had bathed the body of a patient who had just died. As we were turning the patient to wash his back, residual air in his lungs came out in a whoosh. The sound that made was totally unexpected and scared us all. It was a dark night and it was a stressful situation, but still we all had a hard time stifling our nervous laughter. We were relieved when the body was finally delivered to the morgue.

The students were sometimes assigned to work several night shifts in a row. I could never function well after working the night shift. It was hard to sleep during the day because the dorm was bustling with activity. We were still expected to go to classes even after working all night. One day, it would have been better for me to stay up straight through, gone to class, and then gone to bed before going on duty again the next night. I was so exhausted and sleepy that I just couldn't stay awake. I went to my room and put my head down on the pillow for what I thought was just an instant. I ended up sleeping through class and was "put on report" because of it. That meant I was grounded and could not go anywhere but the dorm and the hospital for one month. I had helped staff the hospital on nights like an adult, but now I felt that I was being treated like a child.

The next night, I was on night duty again. When morning came and my shift ended, I stayed up to go to class. The instructor called on me to answer a question. My friends told me later that I fell asleep right in the middle of answering the question and could not be awakened. I had no recollection of the incident, but after completing my required night shift duty, I resolved never to work nights again.

Two of my friends, Dawn and Nancy, loved working nights. After graduation, one worked nights in obstetrics and the other worked on the surgical floor. I was never able to sleep during the daytime, so it was impossible for me to function on night duty.

Chapter 20

Delivering Care

Classes were held Monday through Friday. The students continued to work 40 hours per week in the hospital in addition to attending classes. We worked eight-hour days on the weekends. This was in the early 1960s, of course, before anyone thought of the long hours as exploitation. Because the students worked so many hours in the hospital, we were able to put our book learning into clinical practice almost immediately. We learned about bone fractures and traction and were able to apply what we learned when we went to work on the orthopedic floor.

There were patients who had surgery for hemorrhoids. Back in those days, the sitz bath chair was used in the patient's recovery. The students learned how take care of the hemorrhoidectomy patients and administer the sitz bath. We learned how to professionally care for men as well as women. That was quite a feat, considering we were barely 18 when we began our floor duty in the hospital. Many of the men made sexist jokes as they were being cared for. The students learned to ignore the remarks and carry on with their nursing care.

Many of the patients on the medical floor were elderly and needed lots of hands-on care. There were a lot of stroke patients who were there just before going to the nursing home. They required total care. The immediate treatment and rehabilitation available now was not available at Rehtlaw Hospital in the early sixties. The students simply gave the patients the best nursing care they possibly could.

There were also a lot of cancer patients. Again, the early detection we have today was not available then. Surgical procedures were not as refined as they are now, so the students just gave the best nursing care they possibly could. It was difficult to see patients dying of cancer.

Cardiac care was much different also. The cardiac medications of today were not available at that time. There were no cardiac monitors. The treatment for a "heart attack" was three to four weeks of bed rest.

Ben Matkin was one of those who had suffered a cardiac arrest, or a "heart attack" as it was called then. He was only 33 years old, was handsome and very charming. He was placed on complete bed rest for one month. During that time, he became a favorite of the students. They hovered over him, giving bed baths and bed pans. Every meal was brought to him on a hospital tray. I'm sure it was a long month for him. There were no televisions in the rooms at Rehtlaw Hospital. Ben was probably very worried that his four weeks in bed might not be enough to restore him to good health again.

Finally, Ben was allowed to sit on the side of his bed, a procedure that was called dangling. He then graduated to assisted ambulation when the students walked with him down the hallway and back to his bed. One day, when I was assisting Ben in getting out of bed, he first sat up on the side of the bed. Then he put his feet on the floor getting ready to stand. I put my shoe next to his foot when I stood next to him as I was getting ready to help him stand.

Ben looked down at the floor to get his position stabilized. Then he said rather dryly, "Your feet are bigger than mine."

Couldn't be! But sure enough, my size 10 shoes were just a smidge larger, or at least the large white nurses' shoes were larger than Ben's slippers. Ben laughed, but it was a surprise to me. I knew I had large feet, but this was embarrassing. It was the first time I saw that my foot was actually larger than a man's foot. It didn't bother Ben. He thought it was hilarious.

At the end of the month, after proper reorientation to walking, getting up to the bathroom, and feeding himself, Ben was discharged. Walking up and down the halls and getting back to the activities of daily living constituted his cardiac rehabilitation.

Ben invited all the students to his apartment. He was so grateful for the care he had received that he wanted to treat us. Fraternizing with a patient was clearly against the rules of the school of nursing. Students were not to associate with or date patients, but there were enough students invited that the invitation clearly could not be considered a date.

Ben's roommate served the students screwdrivers. The drink was made with vodka and orange juice. The drinking age in Illinois at the time was 21, so serving liquor to minors would have been the second infraction at this party. Not being an experienced drinker, I downed several screwdrivers. Everyone was standing around talking and laughing. Suddenly, the vodka hit me straight-on, making me dizzy. I had to ease myself down to sit on the floor. There were more people than chairs, so others were already sitting on the carpeted floor. That was my first introduction to hard liquor. After that, vodka would never be my drink of choice.

Chapter 21

The Cab Driver

Our laughter was almost louder than the train whistle as we pulled into Chicago's Union Station. Four of us had just come back from the spring formal at the men's college my boyfriend, Dave, attended. I had been able to see him all weekend. The other girls were able to see their boyfriends, too. Four girls traveling together in 1963 felt perfectly safe. We would take the L (elevated train) back to the suburbs.

I would ride the L a short distance with the other three girls and then get off to catch a bus to the Rehtlaw School of Nursing. From the first bus, I would transfer to the Division Street bus, which would take me to my destination. I planned to walk the two blocks from the Division Street bus stop to my dorm.

It was late at night by the time I got off the L. Up to that point, there had been four girls traveling together. Now it was just me with my large suitcase and purse in the big city at almost midnight.

I got on the bus at the foot of the L platform with no problem. But when I got to Division Street, it took longer to get a bus. Buses didn't run real often after 10 p.m., so I waited a long time. As I walked around with my suitcase, shifting my purse from one shoulder to the other, a cab pulled up to the street corner. The driver, a black man, pushed open the door on the front passenger's side of the cab. At this point in history, a black man telling a white woman to get into his car was a bigger deal than it would be today.

"Get in!" he commanded.

Trying to evade getting in the cab, but trying not to be rude, I stalled.

"I can't," I said, "I don't have any money."

"Get in!" he repeated. "You can pay me when we get to your destination. You shouldn't be standing out on the street corner alone this late at night!"

He was so insistent that I got in, hoping my roommate would lend me the money when I got to the dorm.

"What are you doing out on the street this late at night by yourself? The cab driver continued to scold me. "You shouldn't be doing this. It's too dangerous for a young woman like yourself."

I told him my story and that I had spent all my money on the trip. He drove me to the nurses' dorm. The ride took only minutes compared to how long the bus ride would have taken.

"I'll be down as soon as I can," I promised the driver, hoping he wouldn't mind the delay.

I grabbed my suitcase and purse, and got out of the cab, running as fast as I could toward the front door of the dorm. I put down my suitcase to unlock the door. As I did, I looked at the street.

The cab was gone.

I hadn't heard it drive away. The dorm was on a dead end street, so I would have heard the cab as it made the turnaround.

The next morning, when I told my roommate the story, Mary first berated me for being so foolish, standing on the street corner so late at night.

"Why didn't you take a cab home in the first place?" she asked.

"I didn't have any money left," I said.

I was young and from a small town. I didn't really understand what all the fuss was about. My biggest consideration at the time was how to make my way home.

Later, I realized the dangerous situation in which I had placed myself. I also wondered, "Was he really a cab driver? Or did he come and leave on angel's wings, sent by my Heavenly Father to take care of me when I didn't even know that I needed protection?"

Chapter 22

An Affair

One or two of the upper class students were going out with doctors who were married men. Everyone in the dorm seemed to know about these secret dalliances. News of these relationships spread quickly through the dorm and were whispered about by everyone. One student came back to the dorm with a piece of jewelry that her doctor friend had given her.

I was very bothered by single nurses having relationships with married doctors. I was very naïve. I just kept wondering to myself, "How does a doctor make his choice as to which nurse to date? How does a nurse make her choice as to which doctor to date? Doesn't anyone hold marriage sacred?"

Then one day it happened. The situation presented itself to me.

Dr. Eduardo had just done mouth-to-mouth resuscitation on an infant with meningitis. The child had stopped breathing and efforts to clear the airway had been unsuccessful. Dr. Eduardo simply took the child, cradled it in his arms and breathed into its mouth. The child coughed and began to breathe. I found this incident miraculous, dramatic and very moving.

Later, when I was assisting Dr. Eduardo with starting an intravenous line, I asked him, "Why did you put yourself in the position to contract such a contagious disease as meningitis?"

"When a life is at stake – in this case the child stopped breathing – you can't stop to think of yourself. You must save that life," he said

I was in awe and very impressed. When doctors and nurses work so closely together in life and death situations, there is a strong bond that forms between them. Thrilled with what I had just witnessed, I went on about my student assignment for the day, going into the linen room to pick up the sheets and pillowcases for the beds I needed to make for my patients.

As I turned to leave the linen room, Dr. Eduardo was standing very close to me. He had come in very quietly and I had not heard him come in because I was so intent on my task. He leaned down and his lips met mine in a soft kiss.

"Could this have just happened to me?" I thought.

I was so stunned that I hurried out of the linen room and went quickly to work attending to my patients.

Dr. Eduardo was a very attractive Latino man. He had been a doctor in Cuba, but when Fidel Castro had taken over the government, the pay he received was so low he couldn't feed his family. He could make more money driving a taxi cab in Cuba than he could make working as a doctor in the government hospital. He came to the United States to make a better life for himself. His medical degree from Cuba was not recognized in the United States, so he was working as a resident at the hospital in Chicago until he could pass his medical board exams to become a fully certified physician in the U.S.

He was very charming and flirtatious. His advances set off a string of emotions in me unlike anything I had ever felt before. But he was a married man. I would have to deal with these emotions over the next three years. I was dating Dave and writing letters to him almost daily. Dr. Eduardo had a wife and a child.

Dr. Eduardo would approach me whenever he saw me. In his charming way, he would tell me how beautiful I was. He would get very close to me and put his arm around me whenever he could. It was not unpleasant. No one had ever paid so much attention to me like this before. It would have been very easy to succumb to this tenderness, charm and attention. Instead, I chose to fight against the emotion, to stay pure, and to stay out of the hands of a married man. It would have been very easy to begin an affair.

Dr. Eduardo was kind in that he did not make any more overt advances and he did not ask me out on a date. Instead, the whole thing became an affair of the heart. I struggled with the physical attraction and my feelings for Dr. Eduardo. I had many sleepless nights because of this.

Mary, my roommate, told me how stupid I would be to let this little flirtation get out of hand. "If you give in to him," she said, "you will be no better than the students we have criticized for dating married doctors."

Finally, I heard that Dr. Eduardo's wife was having a baby. She was in labor at our hospital. The next time I saw Dr. Eduardo, I got up my courage and asked him, "How can you continue this flirtatious behavior when you have a wife and a new baby?"

He said, "I am 35 years old. Marriage can lose its luster and one can get bored with life. When you are 35 years old, you will understand."

The next day, I was on duty in the hospital and happened to be walking past the elevator. The elevator door opened briefly and there was Dr. Eduardo, standing in the elevator holding his new baby. His wife and little girl were standing beside him. He was taking his wife home from delivering their second child.

Seeing Dr. Eduardo with his family, I could only imagine how much more of a struggle it would have been if we had fallen into a real affair. I was fortunate that Dr. Eduardo had not pressed me to do so.

Now I could see how these relationships "happen." I now also knew what one needs to do to stay out of such situations. I thanked God for my strong Christian upbringing and continued to try to lead my life in a way that I knew would be pleasing to God, no matter what the temptations.

Chapter 23

Maybe Nursing Isn't For Me

After learning to give injections, seeing death, taking care of cancer patients, working many weekends and holidays, and having such enormous patient loads, I was beginning to feel that nursing really wasn't for me. Nothing about it seemed to suit me. I didn't like the medical floor. I didn't like passing medications. I didn't care for pediatrics, and psychiatric nursing wasn't a favorite of mine, either.

I felt like quitting at the end of my second year in nursing school. The problem was that I didn't want to go back home. I had no money and I didn't know what else I wanted to do if I quit nursing. I decided not to quit, but to finish the course before I went in search of something else.

Then a beautiful thing happened. We began our obstetrics rotation. Here, at last, was something I liked – I mean, really liked. I loved seeing the miracle of a new birth when a new baby was delivered. I liked caring for young mothers who were basically healthy except for recovering from their delivery. They recovered quickly and were soon ready to go home. I liked caring for the babies in the nursery.

The staff nurses in Labor and Delivery and in the Nursery saw how happy I was there. They had a need for someone to work in the nursery to fill in so the nursery staff could take vacation days that summer. They asked me if I would like to come and work in the nursery during my summer break. Would I!! I could think of nothing I would like better. It was pure bliss for me just thinking about it.

I had to get permission from the director of the school of nursing to work in the hospital during my summer break. She readily gave her permission.

The nursing school did not allow the students to stay in the dorm during the four-week summer break. But one of the staff nurses in the nursery, Connie Rehm, invited me to stay with her in her apartment during the weeks I worked in the nursery. I slept in her guest bedroom. Her apartment was within walking distance of the hospital, so it was easy for me to walk to work.

The pay for students who worked for pay on their summer break was minimum wage, about 75 cents an hour. By the end of the summer, I had made enough money to buy a pair of contact lenses. We were required to wear masks in the nursery and in the delivery room during the delivery of a new baby. My glasses kept fogging up in the summer heat and humidity when I wore the masks. With contact lenses, I didn't have to wear my glasses anymore and didn't have to worry about them fogging up.

Now I was all set to apply for a job in Labor and Delivery when I graduated.

Chapter 24

Pediatric Affiliation and a Bathroom Secret

Before I could graduate and seek a position in Labor and Delivery, I still had to go on my pediatric affiliation as well as my psychiatric affiliation. Peoria, Illinois, was the place for the pediatric affiliation for my group. I went there with my first group of six, even though I was now closer socially to Mary, Lila and Victoria. My group of six stayed at the Catholic hospital there and studied pediatric nursing for three months. We were housed in the nurses' dormitory on the top floor in rooms under the eaves that were set aside for students from out of town.

Officially, I was still assigned to my original group of six for clinical studies. It was a bit strange for me to be separated from my gang of Mary, Lila and Victoria. But thankfully, Wanda from my group had agreed to room with me. Wanda was kind to me and remained completely neutral, even though Millie was still giving me the silent treatment. Wanda seemed unaware of the rift between Millie and me. Millie talked to everyone else, but wouldn't even look at me.

There was enough going on at the hospital and the school of nursing during the pediatrics affiliation that I simply ignored Millie. The pediatric patients were challenging and the instructors made our classes interesting. No one seemed to be aware of Millie's treatment of me. There were also students there from two other schools of nursing. I made friends easily and became friends with many of the students from the other groups.

The Peoria School of Nursing hosted several parties and invited students from nearby Bradley College, so there were college men to meet as well. Millie continued her silent treatment, but only she and I seemed to be aware of it.

It was 1964. Barry Goldwater and Lyndon Johnson were running against each other in the presidential election. I was a year older than most of my classmates and was eligible to vote. James, a male nursing student from one of the other schools, was also old enough to vote. A person needed to be 21 to vote in 1964. James and I went together to the polling place set up on campus for the students to vote. I was excited to be able to vote for the first time, but I felt a little odd being the only one in my own nursing school group who was eligible to vote. It was also strange not going to the polls with my parents for this huge milestone event of voting for the first time.

While I was in Peoria, I received word that my mother was to have surgery in a few days. On the day of the surgery, I was so anxious that I didn't feel well. Wanda gave excuses for me when I stayed in bed and missed class. Later that day, the nun who was my pediatrics instructor came to my room. The nun had received word that my mother had suffered a cardiac arrest on the operating table. The medication that was given for the spinal anesthesia had put her into shock. Thankfully, they were able to give a second medication to reverse the anaphylactic reaction, and my mother was alive and recovering. The instructor had been kind enough to deliver the news to me in person so that she could be of emotional support.

Being away from home and not being able to be with my mother when she was sick was unsettling. I couldn't sleep that night and walked down the hall to go to the bathroom. No sooner had I closed the door to the bathroom stall when I heard two voices. One was Millie's and the other was Jessie's, another girl from our group.

"Are you sure?" asked Jessie incredulously.

"Yes, I've missed three monthly periods already," said Millie.

I couldn't see the girls, but I certainly recognized their voices.

"Wait," said Millie, "I think someone is there in the stall. Oh, no. Now my secret is out!"

They could see my feet peeking out from under the door of the stall. They recognized my slippers. I was very surprised when someone else came into the bathroom that late at night and didn't realize quickly enough that they thought they were alone. If I had realized this, I could have lifted my feet so they would not have been seen under the door of the stall. Instead, I kept very quiet and waited until they had gone to their rooms and closed their doors, each of them to their own room.

I was sure Millie thought I would tell everyone the secret I had just heard. It was a very surprising admission by Millie, but I had no intention of being any part of it by telling anyone. Millie would have enough to deal with without me complicating things further by broadcasting the secret.

Millie made it to the end of the term and then dropped out of school. At that time, in the early 1960s, nursing students at Rehtlaw School of Nursing were not allowed to be married or pregnant while they were in school. These two things were grounds for dismissal.

Millie came back to Rehtlaw School of Nursing after my class had graduated. She took her last semester courses with the underclass students and then graduated with that graduating class.

I never told anyone the secret I had heard that night. I never mentioned to Millie or Jessie that I had heard them talking in the bathroom that night. They never mentioned the incident to me, nor did they threaten me so that I would keep the secret quiet.

I could only imagine the constant uneasiness they both felt wondering, "Will she tell or won't she?"

Chapter 25

Jacksonville Psychiatric Affiliation

Our group was now well into our second of three years of nursing school. We went to school year round with only an official summer break and a short break at Christmas. After going home for Christmas, we returned briefly to Rehtlaw Hospital and then prepared to leave for three months of psychiatric study at the state mental hospital in Jacksonville, Illinois.

There, we learned the basic psychiatric diagnoses and worked with patients who were classic examples of these diagnoses. We were not required to wear our student uniforms at the psychiatric hospital and we were not required to give medications to the patients. The medications were given by the regular full-time staff. It was the role of the students to talk with the patients and observe their behavior. In this way, the students could see how the conversation and behavior of the mentally ill patient differed from that of a person who did not have a mental disability.

The students were housed in a brand new dormitory that was within walking distance of the psychiatric hospital. There were students from several other nursing schools represented there as well. The students were arbitrarily assigned to a roommate from a different school of nursing. Students in each set of two rooms shared a common bathroom that was between their dorm rooms. To have only four people to a bathroom was pretty luxurious for our group. Back at the dorm at the Rehtlaw School of Nursing, six or eight students shared a bathroom. One of the students from my group, Wanda Barkley, was assigned to the room on the other side of the bathroom from me. My roommate, Bonnie, was cute, kind and friendly. Bonnie spent most of her time with her friends from her own school, but she always nice to me and treated me as a friend, even though we had never met before. We often studied together in the room that we shared.

That any studying at all was accomplished was truly amazing, because there was always so much activity going on in the dorm with so many students living there. The night before our final, we found it particularly hard to concentrate. It was Sunday night and the Ed Sullivan Show was on the TV in the lounge not far from our room. The volume was turned all the way up because everyone was watching the show. The Beatles had flown from Liverpool to be on the show and were performing that night. Everyone wanted watch them. They had become such a popular singing group, but no one knew at the time just how popular they would become. In spite of all the commotion and lack of concentration, we all passed our exams.

We wore our regular clothes when we went over to the hospital to interact with the patients. It was thought that the patients would respond better to us this way than if we were wearing our student nurse's uniforms.

Once or twice, we were assigned to observe shock treatments given to patients. These treatments were very hard on the patients and very difficult for the students to watch. At that time, no sedation was given to the patients, and the patients could remember the convulsions that happened to them during the treatments. It was not a pleasant thing to see. I found it rather barbaric.

Hydrotherapy was another patient treatment observed by the students. The patients were placed in a bathtub, and many streams of water were applied to the patient from shower-like nozzles. The treatment was rather frightening to the patient during the actual application of water. After the treatment was complete, however, the water therapy appeared to have had a calming effect on the patient.

Some of the patients that we talked with were paranoid. One man was certain that the Russians had planted a listening device in one of his teeth. He had all of his teeth removed to make certain he was free of the listening device, because he didn't know which tooth held the device. Some of the patients were obsessive compulsive and wrung their hands continuously or repeated the same words over and over. The students observed one or two patients in a catatonic state. The patients were immovable, like statues. Nothing could be said or done to them that would make them move or respond. These patients were severely ill. The students were not allowed to talk with them and were only allowed to observe.

Unlike the nurses' residence, which was very new, the hospital that housed the patients was very old. All doors were locked at all times so patients could not walk out onto the grounds and get lost. Also, they could not accidentally walk outside in the winter and suddenly be out in the below-zero weather without coats. These locked wards were presumably for the protection of the patients, but to me it seemed that it was really to protect the neighboring community from unwanted contact with the patients.

Once the students entered the hospital doors, the doors locked behind them. We could not get out without one of the staff letting us out. It was a frightening feeling, but it gave the students an idea of how the patients must have felt being locked inside the hospital every minute of their time there. Further into the hospital, there were wards that one could not enter unless one was admitted by a staff member with a key. When the students were admitted to a ward like this, they were doubly locked in. When I entered even the first set of doors and heard them lock behind me, I had this sinking feeling in the pit of my stomach. It was a brief instant in which I feared that I may never return to the freedom of the outside. I could only imagine how the patients felt. It was virtually like a prison. Supposedly, most of the patients were so mentally ill that they didn't know they were locked in. I never did ask any patient outright how they felt about being in a locked ward, but more than one patient expressed the wish to be released from this hospital prison.

The food at the mental hospital dining room was not as good as the food at Mr. Chaus' dining room. Here there were enormous pots of oatmeal for breakfast. Thankfully, there was also toast and jam, which made breakfast at least palatable. Lunch was mostly soup, again served from large kettles, and there was the ever-present bread and butter for making a sandwich. The evening meal was again basic and plain. Meatloaf was served often with mushy potatoes and vegetables.

The students were allowed to take their trays back to the nurses' residence, which we often did; at least that broke up the monotony of the dining room, the days with patients that were not in touch with reality, and the being away from our own school of nursing.

Dave came to visit me while I was at the state mental hospital. We had a really great time, although there was not as much to do as in Chicago. Parting was very difficult for us. I realized I would miss Dave more than I thought, and that our relationship was getting more serious.

Chapter 26
We Live in the Apartment

Finally, in the spring of our senior year in nursing school, our third year, all the students were back from their affiliations and there wasn't enough room for all of us to live in the dorm.

By that time, I had informally talked to Mrs. Redken, the head nurse in obstetrics, about working in obstetrics on fifth floor after graduation. She actually asked me if I would be interested in working with her at Rehtlaw Hospital in obstetrics when I graduated.

I couldn't believe what I was hearing and stammered, "I would love it!"

That was my interview, and that is how I came to work in obstetrics after graduation.

Mary had requested to work on the medical floor and Lila had requested to work on the post-surgical floor. We three were told we could live in the second-floor apartment of the building owned by the hospital, right across the street from the hospital's side door. We could live there rent-free while we were students.

Now, and later when we were graduate nurses, we went to work simply by going down the stairs of our apartment building, crossing the street, and entering the hospital through the same side door we always entered when we lived in the dorm. It was convenient and a very short commute.

When we graduated, the hospital charged us each $125 per month for rent.

Chapter 27

She's Married?

I didn't know before that night in the bathroom that Millie and Jessie were confidants. Later, we found out that Jessie also had a secret she had been keeping. At that time, Rehtlaw School of Nursing had a policy that students could not be married or pregnant. Both were grounds for dismissal.

Graduation Day for me and my classmates was September 4, 1965. All our families came for the graduation including, this time, mine. Even so, the students were still required to ride to and from the graduation on the bus. The nursing school hired the bus for these occasions so that the whole student body could arrive together at Mt. Horeb Church, where the graduation service was to be held.

It was a beautiful graduation ceremony on a beautiful fall day. The students were all so happy that the graduation ceremony was over and they had finally graduated.

Everyone boarded the bus. There was a lot of loud joyous laughing and talking. Suddenly, a great cheer went up from the back of the bus. Jessie had just told everyone that she had been secretly married. Her boyfriend, Miles, had been drafted and had been called up to Vietnam. Jessie and Miles had been secretly married before he went to Vietnam, but she hadn't been able to tell anyone for fear of dismissal from the nursing program. Now that she had her diploma, she was free to joyously tell the news that she was married.

I guessed that Millie already knew, and that Jessie had told Millie her secret that night in the bathroom when I had overheard them talking.

Chapter 28

After Graduation

After graduation, I went to work as a graduate nurse in Labor and Delivery. I worked the evening shift, which was 3 in the afternoon until 11 at night. Two wonderful nurses worked with me: Mrs. Rubio and Mrs. Lorenzo. I worked full time and they each worked part time, so I got to work with each one of them. Both women were Rehtlaw graduates and very strong Christians. We had a lot in common. They were young mothers and during the shifts that we were not busy, we had time to talk as we worked together. We talked about life, marriage, having children and raising children. I credit them with giving me very good insight into how to live in a committed Christian marriage, how to be a Christian parent, and how to love your spouse and children as well as yourself. It was a good time in my life.

There was also a Filipino nurse who worked with us, Mrs. Fuliga. She was the wife of Dr. Fuliga, a doctor who was a resident also working at Rehtlaw Hospital. She was very nice and a very good nurse. We all worked together so well that I didn't know until I took another job a year later that not all nursing teams work so well together.

Mrs. Gorse worked in the nursery. She was older than the rest of the veteran nurses. She was a widow and kept to herself. She was very moody and sometimes difficult to work with. Mrs. Fuliga covered the nursery on the nights Mrs. Gorse was off.

I remember the freedom I had. I was doing what I loved and I was actually getting paid for it. I was earning my own money and I could spend it any way I wanted. I had made it. I had graduated.

Mary, Lila and I all worked the evening shift. Sometimes when we got off work at 11 o'clock, we would order pizza and watch movies on television all night. We would sleep until noon and then get up and get ready for work. We would go over to the snack bar at the gift shop in the hospital, have a sandwich and then go to work.

Sometimes, especially on payday, we would take the bus into downtown Chicago for a day of shopping. With my first paycheck, I bought a beautiful burgundy-colored mohair coat for winter. In the years I was a student, all I had for winter was a fleece-lined trench coat. It was so exciting to have a nice, dressy wool coat. I bought some other nice clothes, too, but I continued to sew some new clothes as well, buying different and interesting material for the garments I sewed. Before, I had sewn clothes mostly using cotton cloth. Now I made a white mohair top and skirt for myself for Christmas. I also sewed an empire waist dress for my sister because she was still a student and I knew she didn't have many nice clothes. The top of her dress was white mohair and the skirt of the dress was a burgundy suede material.

We made most of our own meals. When we went to the grocery store, we pooled our money and bought food that we liked. We bought some steaks, good fruit, and delicious snacks. Mary knew that I liked shrimp cocktail. She would buy shrimp cocktail for me as a special treat.

"Everyone should have this chance to do just what they please," I thought.

Even with all this new-found freedom, we still worked about three weekends a month. It was rare that the three of us had a weekend off together, unless we specifically requested it.

Chapter 29

Angel Mechanic

After my encounter with Dr. Eduardo, I now had a better idea of how those other nurses and doctors might have come to be in relationships with one another. But no matter how important a man is, he does not have the right to take advantage of a young woman and force her into a relationship she may regret years later, and may prevent her from having a great relationship with her future husband. A young woman in a moment of weakness may enter into a relationship she may regret later.

Dave and I were now very serious. The nurses who worked with me in Labor and Delivery thought Dave would give me an engagement ring at Christmas. Dave was working as a student intern in Michigan. He had a car at his disposal through his internship, so he loaned his own car to me so I wouldn't have to walk to North Avenue to buy groceries and carry them home.

I drove Dave's car back to Chicago after visiting him for the weekend. I parked the car on the street for the night. That night there was a 10-inch snowfall, one of the biggest snowstorms Chicago had seen in years. There was blowing and drifting snow and subzero temperatures. The next morning when I tried to start the car, the engine wouldn't turn over. Frantic, I got the phone book and looked up the nearest auto mechanic. The mechanic said he would be over to look at the car as soon as he could. He said it would not be until that afternoon since he had so many calls just like mine because of the snowstorm.

Late that afternoon, the mechanic arrived to look at the car. The battery was dead because of a loose connection in the radio. I hadn't turned off the radio before turning off the car, and the radio had continued to drain the battery even though the car was turned off. I hadn't expected to pay for a service call as well as a new battery, but I gulped and asked the cost of the service call.

The mechanic looked at me and said, "There is no charge for you. You gave me such good care when I was in the hospital that the service call and the battery are free to you."

I never forgot a face. I had never seen this man before. I would have remembered him if I had taken care of him as a patient. I asked my roommates if they remembered a patient who was an auto mechanic at A-1 Auto Repair Garage. No one else remembered him either. Was he really a former patient? Was he really a mechanic? Or had he, too, come on angel's wings to help me in this emergency situation? God had cared for me when I was a student. Now He was continuing to care for me as I was beginning my life as a graduate nurse.

Dave did ask me to marry him that Christmas. The date was set for late August. Until then, I continued to work at my job in Labor and Delivery.

Early one morning, the phone rang in the apartment. "Ruth, are you and Mary OK?" Dave asked.

"Of course we are OK," I replied, "Why are you asking?"

"I heard on the radio that some nurses in Chicago have been murdered!" he said.

That morning Richard Speck had overcome eight student nurses and murdered them in their dorm on the South Side of Chicago. Dave was calling to find out if we were all right.

We were all right, but now we were very frightened. That night, Mary went to bed carrying a cast iron frying pan. "What are you going to do with that?" I asked her.

"I'm not taking any chances," said Mary. "That guy is still at large." The murders had happened on the South Side and we lived on the North Side of Chicago. I thought we were safe, but Mary wasn't taking any chances.

The untimely death of the student nurses was not the only news story that happened that spring. As spring turned to summer, tension in the city rose and gave way to race riots. Dave and I came back from my parents' home for the weekend. We had been making plans for our wedding. On our way into Chicago, many streets were closed and police squad cars blocked the intersections with their blue lights flashing. One evening, my nursing assistant was late for her shift. It was about the third time in a week and I was not happy about it. When the woman finally arrived, I confronted her.

The woman broke down in tears. "You try getting to work on time when you have to lie on the floor of the bus while bullets are flying through the windows."

Dave took me to my apartment. He was very worried about me and hated to leave me, but he had to get back to his job. He returned several weeks later and helped me move out of my apartment. I resigned my position in Labor and Delivery at Rehtlaw Memorial Hospital. I would be taking two weeks' vacation, at the end of which we were to be married. I would be looking for a new job in the city where we would live.

Chapter 30
Lila Enlists

When we were students and were not on duty, we had a lot of fun. Some of it was fun just being together and laughing and talking. The upper classmen seemed to go out to more parties than our class. They drank a lot, and when they got back to the dorm they played tricks on each other. One trick was to put Saran wrap on the toilet seat so that the person who had too much to drink had a real mess, because they didn't notice that their seat had been altered. Another trick was to put shaving cream inside a manila envelope and put the opening of the envelope under the door of the targeted person. Then the perpetrator would stomp on the envelope and the shaving cream would go flying into the victim's room. This was nursing humor.

There were organized parties in the dorm also. There was usually a fall dance in the lounge on the lower level of the dorm, as well as a Valentine's Day dance. Young men from ITT Technical Institute and DeVry University were invited to come to these dances. The student nurses met some nice young men, as well as some that were not so great.

There was one guy who drove his father's Cadillac and was a big spender. He was always looking for a student nurse to go out with him. Anyone who went out with him usually found that he talked only about himself and was not very interesting. He usually could not get anyone to go on a second date because word spread quickly about what he was like.

One young man asked me out on a date. He and his buddy took Mary and me on a date to the Brookfield Zoo. It was fun and he was very nice, but I kept thinking about Dave the whole time.

Mary finally met a young man she loved and was dating him exclusively. I was engaged to be married to Dave. Lila hadn't really met anyone who interested her, but she had been thinking about enlisting in the Air force. Lila really wanted to enlist, but she didn't want to go to the Air Force recruiting office in downtown Chicago alone, so she talked me into going with her.

We went downtown together so she could fill out the recruiting forms. However, the recruiting officer would not allow me to be there also unless I filled out the recruiting forms, too, so that's what I did. Both of us then had to submit to physicals and the preliminary injections required for new recruits. Lila and I were the only new nursing recruits that day. We had to walk from the physical room to the place where the injections were given. We were unceremoniously wrapped in sheets and escorted past hundreds of male recruits to the place where we would receive our injections. The wolf whistles were the loudest we had ever heard. The guys had no sheets to cover them and were just standing there in their skivvies.

Finally, Lila and I were allowed to leave. A few days later, we received a phone call from the recruiting officer. He told us we would receive our officers' commissions in the mail very soon. The certificates of commission soon arrived, and we were now commissioned lieutenants in the U.S. Air Force.

I was able to decline my commission on the grounds that I was engaged to be married. At that time, in that branch of the service, they allowed a person to decline their commission for that reason. I was greatly relieved when the whole thing was over. I would not have wanted to miss my own wedding because I had been posted to an Air Force hospital far from home. Dave later told me if that had happened, there would have been no wedding, ever. He was very angry that I had taken such a foolish chance.

Lila packed her bags and left for her first assignment, a military hospital on a base somewhere in Texas. She was following her dream.

Chapter 31

Encounter with Eduardo

I worked in Labor and Delivery on the fifth floor of the hospital. Labor and Delivery was its own little world because it was a closed unit. A closed unit meant that no one was allowed on the floor except the staff who worked there, the doctors who had patients there, the patients themselves and their husbands. Children under age 12 were not allowed as visitors in the hospital at that time.

The nurses I worked with were fine Christian women. They were married and committed to their husbands. On slow nights, they would talk with me about their home lives, going to church, and raising their families. The rest of the hospital and the doctors could not intrude on this happy idyllic time, or so I thought.

One day, Dr. Jones appeared on the floor at shift change to talk to my supervisor, Mrs. Redkin. As he was leaving, he stopped to greet me. "Hello, Miss Boettcher," he said, "I have some bottles of champagne that I am giving away. Would you like one?"

"Sure," I said, thinking Dr. Jones was just joking.

Later that night, he had a large magnum of champagne delivered to me on the Labor and Delivery floor. When I brought the champagne over to the apartment after my shift, Mary was furious. "Why did you accept that bottle of champagne from Dr. Jones? You know he has a reputation as a womanizer. You have no idea how you will be obligated by accepting that gift." This was a typical comment by Mary.

Nothing ever came of accepting that gift from Dr. Jones, but Mary was right. That could have marked the start of some clandestine activity because of my naivete in accepting a gift. God was clearly watching over me.

Several days later, I was going back to the apartment from the hospital. Lila had enlisted as a nurse in the Air Force and had moved to her new post. Mary was gone for the day. She had a day off and was visiting her family. I had a day off, too, but had gone over to the hospital just to have lunch.

Dr. Perez stopped me in the hallway. Dr. Perez had come over from Cuba with Dr. Eduardo, and they were both working as residents at Rehtlaw Hospital until they could pass their medical exams in the United States.

"Miss Boettcher," he said, "Dr. Eduardo would like to talk to you. Is it OK?"

"I guess so," I said. "What does he want to talk about?"

Dr. Perez didn't answer, so I just kept on walking. I went out the door and crossed the street to the apartment. It was a rainy day and I was very tired. It had been a busy couple of weeks and it would be good to take a nap, I thought. I put on a nightgown and my new bathrobe over it.

"I'll sleep in Lila's bed," I thought. "I sure miss her now that she is gone to the Air Force."

There was a knock at the door. I opened the door as far as the chain latch would allow. There stood Dr. Eduardo. "Can I come in?" he asked.

I unlatched the chain latch and Dr. Eduardo came into the apartment.

"Oh Ruth," he said, "I have missed you so much." He advanced toward me, attempting to take me into his embrace.

"I thought you wanted to talk," I said, suddenly feeling very irritated and deceived.

Furious, I spun Dr. Eduardo around and marched him to the door. I pushed him out the door and locked and chain-latched the door.

I was so exhausted that I fell asleep immediately. I slept all afternoon. It was not until later that I realized that God had been with me in this potentially dangerous situation. Dr. Eduardo was twice my size. If he had been intent on forcing himself on me, I would not have been able to defend myself. I shouldn't have opened the door in the first place. I was too trusting, not realizing what could have happened.

How I had become angry enough to eject Dr. Eduardo from the apartment, only God knows.

Epilogue

I remained in Chicago for one year after I graduated from nursing school and worked as a registered nurse at the hospital from which I graduated. After Dave and I married, I worked another year in obstetrics. He became a pastor and a missionary. We lived eight years in West Africa, where I did some volunteer medical work.

When we returned to the United States, I went on to complete a Bachelor of Science in Nursing degree. I worked in dialysis as a staff nurse, and taught home dialysis and continuous ambulatory peritoneal dialysis. I went on to work in home care and finally worked as a nurse advocate for senior citizens.

I am now retired and live at home with my husband. We have two married daughters and four grandchildren.

My sister, who is a medical transcriptionist, asked me one day, "Why did you go into nursing anyway?" That question was one of the primary motivations for writing this book. I wrote the book for your reading pleasure, as well as to mark the upcoming 50th anniversary of the graduation from the Rehtlaw School of Nursing, Class of 1965.

I hope you enjoyed it, and I would be most appreciative if you could post a review on Amazon. Thank you!

More From Ruth Boettcher

Follow Ruth and her family as they discover the wonders of missionary work in Nigeria in "The Reluctant Companion: One Wife's Journey to Africa." on Amazon at **http://tinyurl.com/lkg8fjh** or by searching "Ruth Boettcher."

Reluctantly, Ruth reasoned that if even one person was saved by her accompanying her husband to Africa, it would be worth it. Celebrate with Ruth as God sustains her in spite of her anger, fears and wariness, and changes and blesses the reluctant companion.

Also please visit Ruth's Author Central page on Amazon

www.ingramcontent.com/pod-product-compliance
Lightning Source LLC
Chambersburg PA
CBHW070109120526
44588CB00032B/1396